Books by Herbert Knapp with Mary Knapp

Red, White, and Blue Paradise:
The American Canal Zone in Panama
(Harcourt Brace Jovanovich: 1984)

One Potato, Two Potato:
The Secret Education of American Children
(W.W. Norton: 1976)

DID YOU SEE THIS?

DID YOU SEE THIS?

Poems to Provoke the Politically Correct

HERBERT KNAPP

Girandole Books
New York, New York
2016

ISBN-13: 9780997164602
ISBN-10: 0997164603

CONTENTS

JOURNALISM

WORDS

HISTORY

EDUCATION

SOCIETY

Political correctness has stifled independent thought, hobbled the economy, turned sexual relationships into minefields of legal liabilities, and neutered stand-up comedy. In response, poetry has clutched its pearls and hidden in its academic parlor. Poets tell themselves poetry is about feelings and the ineffable—eternal things—not transitory political disputes or (OMG) jokes. LOL has no place in the museum of poetry. It was not always so. In a more robust age (when poetry mattered) insulted children didn't run to the teacher but shouted back, "I'm rubber, you're glue; whatever you say bounces off me and sticks to you."—HK

Reaction may be, and in some true sense is, something utterly different from futile dreaming. It is essentially to answer action with action, to oppose to the welter of circumstance the force of discrimination and selection, to direct the aimless tide of change by reference to the co-existing law of the immutable fact, to carry the experience of the past into the diverse impulses of the present, and so to move forward in an orderly progression.

—Paul Elmer More

POLITICS

OUR SITUATION

What can be expected of a nation
whose boast is that it lacks discrimination?

SHADOW-LIGHT

The night is coming on.
Shadows cross the lawn
like sentences explaining things away.
The differences that set apart
right from wrong, head from heart,
heroes from celebrities,
publicity from expertise,
and art from accident are almost gone
differences that once were plain as day.

Feeling myself slip in and out of sight
as I walk through obscurely bright
abstract shapes
of moon-reflected shadow-light,
I greet the ghosts of differences
that haunt the night.

HEY, CAN'T YOU SEE?

We have no right to believe that if anything were different from what it is, anything else would be the same as what it is.—J. McT. E. McTaggart

Up, up, my friend, we're missing the parade.
No? Why not? The fife and drum?
The uniforms? Hey this is not Iran,
Hitler's Reich, or Imperial Japan.
This is America.

So, Jefferson was "really." Is that true?
And Washington? Him, too? Have you considered
the "really" number I could do on you?
Ah, let that pass. But tell me this:
What would you have had those people do?

Wait! Before you speak, think how the flight
of a butterfly in Kansas can
ignite a dust storm in Afghanistan.
Tweak the historical record you'll start up
differences in all directions.

The Indians—what if they'd won? Or the Mexicans?
What if the white tops hadn't rocked and rolled
to Whitman's Mission and to Sutter's Mill?
Would there have even been a Civil War?
And what then of the slaves?

What if we'd let the Kaiser colonize
the Philippines? Or not dropped Little Boy?
Tojo was planning a giant Okinawa.
Think of the final battle inside Troy.
What *then* would the occupation have been like?

Someday we will learn from someone clever
how to pick the fly poop out of pepper.
But good from evil? Never. Just the same
we have to choose. And so, my friend, would you
choose to be interned by us or them?

A citizen of the world? Come off it, man.
You've got U.S.A. all over you.
Hey, Mister American is what you'll hear
anywhere on earth. So pop a beer,
and let's go celebrate our nation's birth.

EIGHTEENTH-CENTURY SAMPLERS

"Did you see this?" I asked,
showing her *The Daily News*.
"They've found another baby in the trash."

"I'm going to the Met this afternoon
to see those samplers. Do you want to go?"

"Why?" I asked but was ignored.
I still don't know.
She hates to sew.

Some of them were done by girls
barely old enough to do their buttons.
One was seven.

"I bet you couldn't get a little girl
to do this stuff today."

"People do what they're expected to,"
she said, then looked at me:
"What's wrong with you?"

SQUINTING IN THE GLARE

Heavily the low sky raining
Over tower'd Camelot.—Alfred Tennyson

Any friend of liberty, he vowed,
he would support, and any foe, oppose.
"We will not count the cost," he said, which showed,
that unlike his opponent, he had class.
The press was wowed.

Reporters clamored for a word or two
from him whom they imagined
could by glamor do
whatever they imagined.
He promised us he'd close the missile gap,
lower taxes, grow the GDP.
And then he promised us the moon.
Reporters turned to watch "the jumpers"
squeal and swoon.

He knew what he could do because his brother
had enlisted numerologists
to poke through piles of figures and discover
plans that the reporters all agreed
were certain to succeed.

At his inauguration
a picture perfect poet rose to read
a poem he'd been up for half the night
getting right.
But something there was that didn't want it read.*
The wind kept grabbing at his manuscript.
The cold turned all his fingers into thumbs.
The sunlight, weakly warm but winter-bright
smeared his page with glare.
So he decided to recite
a poem he had written long before
about colonials
who realized their land through deeds of war.
But poetry no longer spoke to us.

Our best and brightest all agreed
the president loved chivalry
and was a verray parfit gentil knyght,
unlike his predecessor who was clueless,
cultureless, and bland,
grammatically unsure, a dupe
of businessmen he'd let get out of hand.

The press corps strolled about
affecting courtly airs,
while Hollywood dolls and gangsters' molls
paraded past them up the White House stairs.

Secretly the brothers had a bunch
of wisemen in for lunch
to talk about the war in South Vietnam.
The rulers there were brothers, too—
Diem and Nhu—
but not quite up to what they had to do.

So diplomats at dinner winked
at plotters who winked back and shot
the brothers after Mass
then dumped their bodies in a vacant lot
before the windows of our embassy,
where diplomats sat wishing,
wishing, *wishing* they had not.

"Nothing succeeds like successors," quipped
a sniggerman in Washington,
where politicians sipped their scotch then rose
to dilate on dominoes.
They said the new man Fate
had brought up to the plate
was sure to homer with the help
of coaches from the Pentagon and State.
The President would see to it, they said.
"He can set the crooked straight," they said.

But as we watched his motorcade
rolling through the streets of Dallas,
he was shot dead.
His killer, captured, was about to be
questioned by a magistrate when he
was shot dead, too.
The killer's killer, captured, was asked why.
Enraptured by revenge was his reply.
But was this true?
Who knew?

People traded theories with friends.
Professors pointed solemnly to trends.
And lunatics in public institutions
appeared on television with solutions.†

His successor promised to perform
Texas miracles: to win the war
in Asia, do away with poverty,
and build a Great Society
for us to glory in.
But scribes, abruptly old,
wrote only of what might have been.

His brother tried to take his brother's place.
He promised, if elected, to restore
the nation to a state of grace
But then he, too, was shot and died.
"Why?" we asked his killer. "Why?"

11

"The Phantoms," he replied.
"The Phantom jets he promised to the Jews."
But later on he testified
that he could not recall
the incident at all.

Plot-intoxicated children
rocked and rolled, smoked pot, saw through
appearances, were born again, and studied
radical chic,
but nothing that was translated from Greek.

And as they danced and grew their hair,
soldiers sent to lend a helping hand
to brothers fighting brothers were misled
by testwise numerologists who said
their numbers showed
light at the end of the tunnel.

---

*Frost was the first poet to read a poem at a President's inauguration. He planned to read "Dedication," an obsequious poem declaring Kennedy's election was "The greatest vote a people ever cast." Unable to read his manuscript because of the wind and cold, he recited from memory, "The Gift Outright," a poem about Americans who secured their land through "deeds of war." At the time, the Vietnamese had recently "secured their land" by defeating the French. Years later, after the American intervention under Presidents Kennedy and Johnson, they would defeat us. The analogy between "The Gift Outright" and these events is inexact as are all analogies but is inescapable, as is the parallel between the Kennedy and Ngo brothers.

†This confusion was the result of the media's inability to accept that the President was not assassinated by the city of Dallas or by right-wing extremists, but by a Communist,

WE LIVE IN THE SHADOWS

Quand un peuple a de bonnes moeurs,
les lois deviennent simples.—Montesquieu

Congress passed a law the other day
that is longer than *Remembrance of Things Past*
and more opaque than *Finnegan's Wake.*
Our Representatives admit they haven't read it,
which means they didn't write it, either.
We are governed by butlers and upstairs maids.

Restaurants are required to serve us salads.
And we are forbidden to smoke indoors.
But we grow more lethargic every day.
Movie stars and journalists insist
that what's required is plainly more repression,
And so our laws, like kudzu, grow and grow,
and we live in the shadows
of prosecutorial discretion.

NOTHING WORKS

I've tried and tried
to write about the towers burning
and the leapers dropping, dropping,
dropping through the morning light.
But nothing works. The job's too much for me.

And maybe it's too much for poetry
the way it's done today. The subject's like
a sturdy country girl among the sleek
glamazons of Fashion Week.

Oh, she would be a wow
wearing a Kipling or a Julia Howe.
But those styles aren't just dated. They're obscene.
Imagine it. The arts community
would have a cow.

NINE ELEVEN

Pursued by pouncing billows of pulverized cement, the survivors walk back to life, wrapped in ashy cerements, and we hang flags from windows, alarming the manicured mandarins of multiculturalism, who pose before the mirrors of their minds, reflect, and quote: "We must love one another or die."*

Journalists, whose professional commitment to objectivity prevents them from wearing American flag lapel pins, preen and pose and denounce us as flag-wavers, fascists, and jingos. "Come," they cry, "let us Reason together. Do as we say."

But already "the corn is as high as an elephant's eye," and flags are signaling defiance, grief, consolation, despair, pride, fraternity, allegiance, and the end of conversation. Clichés, long thought to be extinct, have come to life: Land of the Free, Home of the Brave, In God We Trust, and Pass the Ammunition.

---

*From "September 1, 1939" by W. H. Auden. After this poem was published, Auden decided this line was "a damned lie" and tried to repair it. Later, he decided the whole poem was "infected with incurable dishonesty" and refused to let it be republished

ELECTION DAY

He openeth his eyes, and he is not.—Job 27:19

Inside the curtained booth, concealed from view,
I do not do what I've come here to do.
Instead, I daydream I'm a volunteer,
onstage inside the box of a magician
whose schtick is he can make me disappear.

"You can't," I tell myself, "stay here forever,"
And so I make my choices, pull the lever . . .
The curtain opens; I step out and see . . .
Just as I feared!
Having voted, I have disappeared.

THE TYRANT

He says he's come to save us, and he loves us.
He says he won't let anything go wrong.
But who knows what he thinks is wrong?
Or who his enemies will be tomorrow?
The Whites, the Greens, or the Dark Blues?
Prudent folk have had their gardens paved.

He says he will deliver us
from all the rules that hold us down,
will liberate our libidos,
and free our verse.
Already he's unleashed his dogs
and opened all the cages of the zoo.

They're coming. Shut the door. Turn off the light.
At least his portrait's out of sight.
My children are infected with his lies,
but trying to make them well would be unwise.
We live or die according to his whim.
What I can't say is like a phantom limb.

HEROES

We don't have plain old heroes anymore.
We've got super heroes. Progress, right?
Sort of like those gods of ancient Greece.
But ours aren't half-divine. They're men who've been
by accident or by design transformed
by mutants, cosmic rays, or a spider's bite.

But they are just diversions—science fictions—
unlike my high school friend I just found out . . .
I went to college while he went to war.
The Medal of Honor. Yes. Big deal. He's dead.
His name is on a list. So what was his
last full measure of devotion for?

And then there is that couple down the block.
They have it all, the looks and the credentials.
They should be going places, but, instead,
they've sacrificed the lives they should have led,
to caring for a child, who should,
if life were fair, be dead.

Well, really, human sacrifice
is just so primitive—so gloom and doom.
I thought it was illegal. I don't know . . .
Just seeing them has got me to the point
where I've postponed my project to redo
the living room.

AN AURA OF OMNIPOTENCE

Augustine of Hippo has confessed
that when he was a boy he climbed a fence
and stole some pears.
And then he threw them all away.
He didn't want the pears.
What he wanted was the satisfaction
of committing an offense.
He wanted to believe he was enclosed
by an aura of omnipotence
and like a superhero lived alone,
costumed and famous but unknown.

THE REFORMER

He bored from within,
got under their skin,
and found he'd become
an opposable thumb.

GOLFING CHUMS

Periodically our politicians
spend enormous sums
to make our dreams come true.
They never do.
All that happens is their golfing chums
pick a few
financial plums.

And when the bums are booted out,
the chums find work for them to do
in companies too big to fail
because they know the bums know all about
keeping thumbs upon the scale.

SAVING THE ESTABLISHMENT

Captured by the enemy,
we died inside the prisons of a friend
whom our policy-wise establishment
believed was too important to offend.

Our liberators locked us up.
Why? I can't be sure.
But we were quarantined for something
with no known cure.

Our diplomats decided
not to make a fuss.
The Soviets, of course,
saw nothing to discuss.

_____

*At the end of the Second World War, thousands of Soviet POWs were in
German camps in the Western zone of Germany. Thousands of American
British, and French POWs were in camps in the Eastern zone. Stalin
demanded the Soviet POWs be sent back to the Soviet Union. They were,
though they resisted going. Some committed suicide rather than go back. The
American, British, and French POWs in the East were not sent to the Western
zone. Stalin denied they existed.*

Soon, alas, it was too late
to admit that we'd been left behind.
We vanished in the fog of war,
Out of sight; out of mind.

We died forsaken far from home
but not for our country.
We died to save the establishment
from embarrassment.

The Washington Post *(July 4, 1991) reported that ex-POWs such as Martin Siegel, who escaped from a Soviet-controlled camp, said many Americans had been left behind but that he had been told to remain silent about this. He was assured it was being investigated. Russian names were reportedly assigned to American, British, and French survivors in the secret Soviet camps. After the collapse of the Soviet Union, Russian President Boris Yeltsin admitted American POWs had been sent to Soviet labor camps.*

YOU NEVER KNOW

A variation of Da bienes Fortuna,
by Luis de Góngora (1561-1625*)*

Life will never go
according to the epistles.
Expecting whistles, flutes.
Expecting flutes, it's whistles.

There seems to be no plan
but merely new digressions.
The state awards a man
both honors and possessions.
So then he spouts confessions
and joins the destitute.
Expecting a flute, a whistle.
Expecting a whistle, a flute.

Sometimes the way it goes,
a guy begins to tell . . .
His wife breaks in and crows,
"I'm pregnant!" "Hey, that's swell!"
They celebrate, what the hell,
ignoring his dismissal.
Expecting a whistle, a flute.
Expecting a flute, a whistle.

25

You see kids go to jail
because they stole a ride,
while men who work wholesale
in fields like homicide
are feted far and wide
and wear expensive suits.
Expecting flutes, it's whistles.
Expecting whistles, flutes.

JOURNALISM

THE JOURNALIST

From 1941 to '43,
a journalist, Kazimierz Sakowicz,
lived in shuttered rooms beside a pit.
The Nazis murdered Jews there every day.
Both children and adults.
He watched them through a slit and kept a score.
He wrote how they behaved and what they wore.

The Romans crucified rebellious slaves
like billboards all along the road
from Rome to Capua.
And after razing Nishapur
the Mongols built a pyramid of skulls
to let whoever still had eyes to see
learn of them and of what they had done.

But that was not the Nazis' way.
So Sakowicz wrote everything on scraps
and buried them in bottles,
knowing if his words were seen too soon,
that he'd be down there with those Jews,
but knowing, too, that this was news
that would stay news.

LIMITS

Inspired by a minor incident in Michael Straight's memoir, After a Long Silence, *p. 201.*

The thought of the disgrace
the nation he'd betrayed would face
if Eleanor served Winston drugstore liquor
caused the crooked Straight to snicker.

But in the end he wasn't tough enough
to turn his back on his old friend,
and so he told his man to send
poor Eleanor a case of decent stuff.

Straight was a friend of Franklin and Eleanor Roosevelt and the publisher of The New Republic *magazine. He was also a Soviet spy. Thirty years after he says he quit spying, he confessed, but then, with the hauteur of the rich and well credentialed, he said he had never been serious about his spying and, thus, had never been a real spy. He threatened to sue any reviewer of his book who called him a spy. He had, however, remained silent for decades about friends of his who were very real, very highly placed Soviet agents. He could not understand that his long silence made him complicit in their activities. The philosopher, Sidney Hook, defied Straight's threats and called him not only a spy but "some kind of zombie." Straight did not sue. The F.B.I. set up a meeting between Straight and Anthony Blunt, the Soviet agent who had persuaded him to become a spy. Straight explained to Blunt that he had confessed because the American government had "finally decided to support the arts." Incredible? Yes, but true. The F.B.I. recorded the conversation. A short time later, President Johnson made Straight the deputy director of the newly formed National Endowment of the Humanities!*

WALTER DURANTY: WINNER OF THE PULITZER PRIZE

Duranty won a prize by writing wrongs
for the *New York Times.*
No journalist has ever hidden
greater crimes.

But since he just repeated
his sources' lies,
the paper says it can't be said he cheated
and won't return his prize.

In his memoir, Zara Witkin quotes Duranty as saying, "What are a few million dead Russians in a situation like this? Quite unimportant. This is just an incident in the sweeping historical changes here. I think the entire matter is exaggerated."

JOURNALISTIC STANDARDS

Any report of a famine in Russia is today an exaggeration or malignant propaganda. —Walter Duranty

Everyone agrees
(seventy-one years later)
Duranty's dispatches
were "gravely defective."
But a committee of his fellow journalists
(seventy-one years later)
convened and could not find
"clear, convincing evidence"
of "deliberate deception."

The committee extended its sympathy
(seventy-one years later)
to everyone affected by
the *Holodomor*, the genocide
Duranty denied and denied,
but decided his lies
were an insufficient offense
to deny him his prize
for journalistic excellence.

THE CONVERGENCE OF THE TWAIN

IN THE SOVIET UNION
Over there
an inconvenient person was unborn.
The books he wrote, the articles that mentioned him,
unwrote themselves.
The photographs of him with friends
were redeveloped and revealed
that no one of his name
existed in the frame.
And prudent people disremembered him.

IN HOLLYWOOD
Over here,
an inconvenient person's born again
on movie screens,
to live and die the way he should.
We understand these things in Hollywood:
The rich are always gangsters in disguise;
patriots are full of lies;
Reagan was a Christian hypocrite,
and Jefferson, a racist shit.

THE ATMOSPHERE IS LIKE A GRAZING DEER

I step out through the door and see
the street is empty and my lawn is wet.
My Maggie's over sniffing at a tree.
Halfway up its trunk a squirrel has stopped.
I look at it; it looks at me.
The atmosphere is like a grazing deer
that senses something and has raised its head.

What have I come out here for?
Oh, yes, the paper. There it is. What's new?
The Red Wings won. We're still at war.
The President's statement turns out isn't true.
I raise my head.

Everything's the same and yet
nothing is the way it was before.

CANDIDE'S ADVICE

I used to read the paper every day.
I made my way through acronyms, unchallenged
lies, and numerous allusions to
actors, athletes, and famous chefs.
It was, I thought, the thing to do.

And almost every day I found a story
whose precious little sense
was hidden in a mist of missing words
lest plainly put it should incense
some tepid terrorist.

What difference does it make if I keep up
with what some trendy journalist has to say?
I am going to take Candide's advice,
which doesn't mean I'm going to disregard
the rumors of war or of insolvent banks.

What it means is I am going to spend
more time in my garden. I intend
to learn the Latin names of all my flowers
so I can greet them properly
and show them I would like to be their friend.

WORDS

A BIG MARKET FOR DEATH

I have seen "a lot" become "alot";
"all right," "alright"; and "crap," respectable.
And I have seen "diversity"
come to mean "conformity,"
and now, alas, "adult" means "pornographic."

The other day I told a man
that in my lifetime songs had gone
from celebrating love to celebrating rape.
And he replied his research showed
"a monster market for that stuff,"
adding as he walked away
before I had a chance to speak,
"It's gonna pay."
Answers only matter to the weak.

Everybody says that life is meaningless.
The planet's doomed, and soon we'll all be dead.
But as my broker's always said,
"Adversity means opportunities."
He wants me to invest in nursing homes
and assisted living communities.

NOT BAD BUT "BAD"

We used to say that what we liked was good,
and that's still true of fruit and vegetables.
But clothes and people that we like are "bad."

Not bad but "bad."
People learning English can't be sure
if they are being had or not.

They soon catch on. The people dressed in rags
who look as if they've stepped out of an ad
are people who are playing being "bad."

It's also possible that someone "bad"
when he or she's not being photographed
is really not so "bad."

But, hey, I'm told it isn't good
to be judgmental.
That's just plain old really, really bad.

BOT SEX

I hear that there's a law (A law no less!)
that "yes" means "yes." Oh, no. It's not
for politicians. It's designed
for college guys with sex in mind.

Like children playing Mother May I.
You remember, "Mother, may I take
two baby steps?" "One giant step?"
Anyhow, according to this law,
each sexual step must be preceded by
a clear request and answered, "Yes."

He asks, "Is it okay to . . ." What? she wonders.
He does, too. His brain is tied in knots.
They didn't start this with a list of wants.
Life is cloudy; clarity's for bots.

PLAYING-LIKE

Language is a guide to social reality.
—Edward Sapir

We used to say that boys were boys
and men were men. No more. Today
men and boys alike are "dudes."
Sometimes even girls are "dudes."

So what? Well, that's what I thought, too,
till I remembered not so long ago
dudes were city folks in cowboy duds
who spent a week or two just playing-like.

And so is dubbing everyone a "dude"
a dodgy way to say that none of us
is being fooled, that all of us
know that the cowboys all have gone away
and that the ranch today
is run by people who are playing-like?

THE SNOW IS ALMOST GONE

Inspired by Horace, IV: 7

The snow is almost gone,
and traffic flows more smoothly now between the banks and stores.
But spring arriving leaves.
Already Macy's mannequins are in their summer clothes.

The tulips in our tree pits
bloom then fall apart as trees form leafy clouds that shade
impatiens forming mounds
that shrivel as the earth receives its crown of leaf-stripped trees.

The world repeats itself,
but you and I, my friend, do not. And if we did, what then?
Why, we'd be different men.
The wordy weather we grew up in will not come again.

We know that when we're dead,
smirking politicians will divide up our "remains"
to finance their campaigns.
A penny spent's a penny saved from them, I've always said.

But time's not ours to spend
or ours to save. It goes no matter what we do or don't
And when its gone: The End.
"Imagine something after death," I tell my mind. It won't.

But haven't there been things
our sages have for centuries agreed could not be true
and then, "Ah-hah! It works,"
in spite of all the sages thought for centuries they knew.

We discover things
that no one could imagine all the time. Your Mom—could she
imagine you? Could you
imagine who, to your surprise (and mine) you've come to be?

To be alive is strange—
stranger than we tend to think and maybe than we can.
But who does not at times
suspect behind its weird, uncanny queerness is a plan?

Just think how strange it is
that like a pair of natural magicians we can shape
words from naught but air
with meanings we can share but can't be taxed by politicians.

Photo by Lee Snider

SOME GUYS YOU JUST DON'T MESS WITH

At the entrance to the New York City
Museum of Natural History
is a statue of a racist,
jingoistic politician
up on his high horse,
attended by "natives" on foot.

Our neo-Calvinist Elect
insisted the commissioners reject
a statue of FDR
holding a cigarette.
Also the one of Eleanor
reminding us she often wore
a stole made from the furry skins
of animals.

But entering or leaving the Museum
of Natural History, the Elect
avert their eyes and hurry by
the statue of the boisterous bully boy,
up on his high horse, lording it over them,
often with a pigeon on his head.

HISTORY

AFTER THE GREAT WAR, 1914-1918

The war that was called Great invades my mind.
—Vernon Scannell

. . . On a huge hill,
Cragged and steep, Truth stands, and hee that will
Reach her, about must, and about must goe.
—John Donne

I don't miss the horses, kings, or corsets.
But are we really better off without
patriotism, rhyme, and inhibition,
classical architecture, and religion?

So why did those things have to go?
Oh, I don't know. The trenches grew into
a maze of open graves, while living men
about them and about them went,

but they, without a hill, made no ascent.
The hill where Truth did dwell had flattened been
by the artillery, and then the rains
of useful lies made muck of the remains.

"What next?' An ad-man answered: "Friend, the truth
is Youth is Beauty; Beauty, Youth.
So purchase any product on this shelf,
apply it and rejuvenate yourself."

"No," cried a Socialist, "I'll rearrange
the world so it will never ever change.
Inside my paradise of repetition,
we'll all be free from death and competition."

"Dada." cried the artist: "Dada! Dada!
Follow me out of your mind!
Unconfined by reason or religion,
we'll be impossible for death to find."

But nothing worked, so all that's left to do
is wander through the mazes of our lives,
dreaming that an earthquake or eruption
will raise a hill above the muck of lies.

OVERHEARD AT LUNCH

A student at the table next to mine
said that his professor said
that stupid people used to think
that we Americans went over there
like superheroes in a comic book
and saved the helpless Europeans.
"Yeah," replied his friend,
"we swooped down from the sky."
They laughed, those two young men—
too wise already to be taken in.

After the Battle of Okinawa
a civilian wept and would not eat.
A Nisei questioned him and said he said
he'd killed his daughters and his wife
to spare them from
the atrocities to come.
Oh, yes, he read the leaflets promising
no civilian would be harmed.
But he was not a fool and had not been
taken in.

THE FALL OF ROME, 1959

We left the children with their grandmother,
went shopping, then came back and found
the table set, which meant
she was expecting us to stick around.

I took my ice cream in the den where Dad
was having televisions. Indians had
a wagon train surrounded, but . . .
Cut to the fort. The hero's gotten through!

"'Sit snowin' yet?" Dad asked. I said it was.
We looked but couldn't see.
The inside light had blacked the outside out,
and so we looked again at the TV.

The chieftain shook his spear. I said, "I hear
the market's similar to twenty-nine."
But Dad said, "Nothing could be sillier."
The whooping Indians formed a battle line.

"Oh stocks will dip." He paused. The Indians charged.
"But not like twenty-nine, not yet.
There is a crash a-comin' though. You bet.
We can't go on a-pilin' debt on debt."

Then he got going on the fall of Rome.
I finally interrupted him to say
that it was late—the kids should be in bed.
"Just you wait! You'll see. Be hell to pay."

While I was wrestling kids into their coats
and boots, he said the danger was as plain
as day. "What don't you understand?" he asked.
My mother ruled the evening had been grand.

I stepped outside and stopped, still warm,
to button up and eye the storm.
"It's slippery," I warned, then led the way,
playing the hero, to our Chevrolet.

By keeping to the ruts, I got us home.
We tucked the girls in bed. "Sweet dreams," we said,
then went downstairs to watch the news and drink
cocoa to encourage sleep.

It said some kids had been caught playing guns
with real ones and that another dumb
celebrity'd OD-ed on drugs. We talked
of what we'd bought and had to buy

to make our lives reflect the lives we'd seen
in magazines and on TV
as snow came down outside like ashes from
Vesuvius.

DON'T ASK ME. I'M ASHAMED.

I'd never dial us back into the past.
Think of the horse plop. Think of the flies. The heat.
Think of sitting on a chamber pot.
And think of your teeth. Why do you think there's not
a single smile in those old photographs?
And don't forget the Civil War.

I read a diary a woman kept
in 1834. She wrote about
her children mainly. She had five.
Then scarlet fever! What to do?
She wiped their faces, prayed, and washed their feet.
A page or two, not one was left alive.

Nevertheless, unlike the future
where know-it-alls appointed by the state
will see to it our cages are kept clean
and we are not unhealthy or unhappy,
the past—the past is something I can love.
Don't ask me. I'm ashamed. I can't explain it

THE FASHIONS OF THIS WORLD

What's left of Freud and of the talking cure
of which so many were so sure?

And what of Marx whose faithful were so certain
that paradise was just behind the curtain?

Darwin is still being taught,
but he is being quietly rethought.

And where is *Colliers?* Where is ten cent beer?
The girls without tattoos of yesteryear?

The world I'm in is not the one I knew
when I was twenty-one in '52.

THE AGE OF REASON

For it is written, I will destroy the wisdom of the wise . . .
1 Corinthians 1:19. (cf. Isaiah 29:14)

The problem with atrocities
is how much sense they make.
Are *you* prepared to stand and say
that making sense is a mistake?

Leszek Kolakowski makes the same point in Modernity On Endless Trial:
" . . . *in the normal sense of 'rationality' the rational grounds for respecting human life and human rights are no greater than, say, for forbidding the consumption of pork among Jews, or meat on Friday among Christians, or wine among Muslims—are they not all 'irrational' taboos? And is not a totalitarian system that treats people as exchangeable parts in the state machinery to be used or discarded, or destroyed according to the state's needs in a sense a triumph of rationality? Still, that system is impelled in order to survive, reluctantly, to restore some of those 'irrational' values. It thus denies its rationality and thereby proves that perfect rationality is a self-defeating goal.*"

FLEEING THE PAST

Fleeing the past that made our parents sad,
we planned to be forever young and glad,

but now, when it's too late, we see
without what was there's no to be.

WITH THE FAST CROWD

We declare that the splendor of the world has been
enriched by a new beauty: the beauty of speed.
—Futurist manifesto, First Series, 1909

Armored with an attitude,
we get into the fast lane, eat fast food,
fast fuck friends, and keep fast answers hot.

We screw our music loud to blast our way
into Nirvana and are proud
of being not

like Mom and Dad.
When we mean something's "good,"
we say it's "bad"

and have no time to find a rhyme,
or count the cost,
or see that what we really are is lost.

As our velocity increases,
faces blur and conversation ceases.
Then a scream erases everything.

EDUCATION

THE GOOD STUDENT

His "child centered" teachers
preached (while reviling preachers)
that he should stay a child like them—
an unappraised and uncut gem.
So to this day, he plays with feelings and words
much like an infant polishing turds.

TWO SYSTEMS

THE ANCIENT CHINESE SYSTEM

Families are encouraged "to have students,"
who, on auspicious dates,
are examined by pontiffs of poetry
and informed of their fates.

Even those who pass cannot be certain
they will receive a spot
in the emperor's administration.
Those who fail are certain they will not.

But pass or fail, they've all become
too proud of all they know
as gentlemen and members of the club
ever to disrupt the status quo.

"Thus things proceed in their circle
and the empire is maintained."

THE AMERICAN SYSTEM

There is an imaginary something
called an education
that children are urged by their betters to buy.
It's so expensive they will probably
be debtors until they die.

A child who isn't old enough
to purchase a cigarette
is permitted to commit himself
to a lifetime of debt.

Why is this encouraged? I don't know.
But debt is a burden, and a debtor
is unlikely to upset the status quo.

"Thus, things proceed in their circle
and the empire is maintained."

THE CRITICAL THINKERS

Since they have been to school, they do not need to wonder, doubt, investigate, or read.

THE REBEL

Free as a bird that goes predestined ways,
he does not know the laws that he obeys.

THE TROUBLE WITH THE BOURGEOISIE

I dress as a boy or girl or an inbetween
and wear my underwear as outerwear.
I refuse to do what you want me to
but you don't care.

You have to respect my freedom of choice.
It's the law. But it isn't fair,
that you only obey—I can tell—because
you don't care.

The only thing you care about is money.
It's the only thing that isn't free,
but it ought to be! It ought to be!
Because if it were I'd live at the Ritz
where I wouldn't care if you didn't care
about me.

THE SOCIAL JUSTICE WARRIORS

"Mirror, mirror on the wall,
who is the most oppressed of all?"
You," says their reflection. "You.
And thus you are entitled to
riot, protest, and denounce your nation
for its lack of dedication
to you, you, you."

SOCIETY

DISCONNECTING DOTS

Contra the serpent's totalizing vision,
its brilliant and unblinking eyes,
that lock its prey in place like a logician,

we've learned, alas, by trial and error
that settled science is sustained
only by trumpets, trolls, and terror.

Wisdom is not found in a conclusion
but in the ever-working mind,
civilizing us with some confusion.

Conclusions tie our minds in knots.
We free ourselves by telling jokes and stories
and disconnecting dots.

HERBERT KNAPP

WHO BELIEVES?

Who can see what happens when
a union's leader tells his men
to "work to rule"
and still believe that rulers can create
a perfect state?
A perfect fool.

PLANET A, REGION 6, ALIEN TYPE 422

The people here are planners.
They do not plan to die so see no need
for children. Actually,
they're not exactly what we'd call alive
but plan to be and know that it's important
to keep the faith while they prepare for life.

So every gesture, word, and look
that might impair their self-esteem is banned.
Experts tell them what to eat and drink
and how much they can weigh,
and other experts full of expertise
decide what they can think and say.
And at the first whiff of imperfection,
their politicians shout, "We've changed direction!"

A BEHAVIOR MONITOR EXPLAINS

Fun! It's the new Core Value.
The cover of the magazine *Inc.*, August 2007

Good citizens need spectacles.
We put them on.
We do it with our technicals.
Just click! Your boredom's gone.

We show you how
the Great Good Place beyond the deeps of air
is coming into being now,
and tell you what to eat and drink and wear.

But sometimes someone's wires get crossed,
and that can't be neglected.
Society will pay the cost,
but must be protected.

O, there's one now. How sad. He cannot "see"
a single joke they're telling on TV.
He's gone outside. He's out there all alone!
I'm trying. He's not answering his phone.

What is he looking at? That tree?
It isn't moving. What's to see?
Poor baby, I remember him when he
was like an opened Coke, so fresh and free.

So hide your eyes inside our spectacle
until we've disconnected him.
Oh, he'll be better off, no doubt of that.
His fizz is flat.

About mercy killing, D. J. Enright wrote: "It is hardly possible to set one's face against the idea of mercy killing. The sacredness of life is too easily, unfeelingly, invoked against it. Yet given so much evidence of a total disregard for that sacredness, one may not want to weaken it further."

I LOOKED INTO MY MIRROR

Man is as if it were two . . . a sort of genius is, with man,
that accompanies him . . . wherever he goes; so that a man
has a conversation with himself, that is, he has a conversation
with his own idea.—Jonathan Edwards

I shun father and mother and wife and brother when my
genius calls me. I would write upon the lintels of the door-
post, Whim. I hope it is somewhat better than whim at last,
but we cannot spend the day in explanation.—Ralph Waldo Emerson

I looked into my mirror. There he was,
so simple, so respectable so dull.
He brushed my teeth and stood up straight.
He paid my bills, let ladies enter first,
and left for work at seven every day.

He wasn't hip. He wasn't cool.
I pitied him. I said, "Hey, Dude,
Why not we loosen up? Come on.
There isn't time for explanation.
Life is short—should be a celebration."

"Go," I told him, "do your thing." He did.
He fled from all the old familiar faces.
He followed his whim.
And as for me, well, naturally,
I followed him.

And now, our coat is torn. Our cuffs are frayed.
And, yes, we're broke, unwashed, unshaved.
But we've been Saved and won't give up.
"Unbleared, unsmeared by toil and trade,"
we rattle our cup.

TOGETHER BUT ALONE

I watch them walking by me hand in hand,
each of them is talking on a phone
while they walk by me hand in hand.

I hear her tell him that she understands,
and see him speak into his phone.
And all the while they're holding hands!

Like two Medusas who are both afraid
that face to face they'll turn themselves to stone,
they live together but exist alone.

Now they're sitting side by side
dancing their thumbs and swiping their little screens,
exploring cyberspace on their machines.

Making choices is their drug.
It makes them feel like they are self reliant
and have no need to pray or dream or hug.

The past, they have no doubt,
is just a sad and boring time without
the choices modern life is all about.

For them there is no greater satisfaction
than that of being constantly
"distracted from distraction by distraction."

When puzzled, they ask Google. (Google knows
everything worth knowing.) When they're sad,
they send each other kitty videos.

THE NUMBER ONE TRAIN, RUSH HOUR, 1995

Pushed on down the aisle
by the incoming crowd at Ninety-Sixth,
I stopped before a seated woman reading,
"HOW TO TEACH THE USE OF CONDOMS."

Upside down, the first subhead declared:
"STRESS THE NEED TO BE PREPARED."
And this was followed by: "TECHNIQUES COMPARED."
And then (It's true.):
"HOW TO HANDLE THE EMBARRASSED STUDENT."
The final section then revealed:
"WHEN A CONDOM SHOULD BE USED."

Looking up she saw what I was doing
and slapped her notebook shut.
So I, no longer smiling, looked
at my reflected face inside the glass
above her head
as we sped through the underworld
to Forty-Second Street.
The local stops kept floating by,
and then beside us on another track,
an uptown train went roaring back.

DID YOU SEE THIS?

Its lighted windows flashed me news.
Of what? Of what?
I couldn't hear
myself think.
But I suspect it had to do
with the existence of another way.

HERBERT KNAPP

TWO THEORIES

*There is no general doctrine which is not capable of
eating out our morality if unchecked by the deep seated
habit of direct fellow-feeling with individual fellow men.*
—George Eliot, Middlemarch

Let's stipulate that we're conceived in sin
and have not got free will, and so cannot
improve ourselves a tittle or a jot.
What would be the point, if that's the case,
to try to make the world a better place?

But what if we can reason right from wrong
and live, if we so choose, without a spot?
Would that not mean it was our duty, friends,
to cleanse the world
of those who would perversely rather not?

Either way, what hope for us? And yet,
Samaritans still stop to help me out;
and I have heard that sometimes true believers,
set to kill, will dazzled be by doubt.

84

A PROBLEM OF COMMUNICATION

They neither deny nor disclose.
They neither support nor oppose.
Having no convictions, they can't see
why everybody can't agree.

"Of course we don't approve of how they treat
women, Christians, gays, and Jews!
But who gives us the right to judge
people with different views?

"'We must love one another or die,'*
like the poem says. So given the stakes,
doesn't that justify excusing
their massacres as mistakes?

"Does it make sense for us to be
overly scrupulous? We simply must—
for the sake of the children—
convince them we are people they can trust.

"So, listen, let's disarm!
Will that not send
a message that we mean no harm
and really, really want to be their friend."

I watch them from afar as they deliver
presents to our enemies then wait,
basking in self-esteem,
for them to reciprocate.

I watch them being forced to kneel.
But they don't stoop to being rude.
Insisting their gesture was misconstrued,
they vow to appeal.

This line is from W.H. Auden's, "September 1, 1939." In 1944, he cut the stanza in which it appeared. Later he judged the whole poem fundamentally dishonest and refused to let it be reprinted during his lifetime. Earlier, in 1940, he had written, "poetry makes nothing happen." Apparently, he had reconsidered that line as well.

A COUNTING RHYME

Cooking the books, the producers peek and
grin at the fans outside who are trying

to get in. The yawning star observes the
scene below and works herself up to make

herself up for yet another show. But,
"No!" her manager says, "That's enough." Can't

close the door is treated rough as people
push inside and him aside and fill the

seats and aisles and more are coming leaping
in the pit the boiling curtain jerks and

opens there they are just staring back and
chewing gum the star arrives she's just a-

nother face in the crowd outside is get-
ting louder hey remember us a scream

a crash no place to go and shouts of FI-
RE what a show this is my friends THE END.

APRIL

Hi, there, April! How's the cruelest month?
Say, I know why we call you that. Don't laugh.
We're all entitled to our theories.
It was the war. The Western Front. All that.
The trenches. The artillery barrages.
The gas. The rats. The mud. The millions dead.
It purged us of illusions, don't you know?
Politics, Religion, and Romance
were crap. So when your lilacs bloomed as if
you didn't give a damn what we'd been through,
we said, okay, to hell with Beauty, too.
That left us only Alcohol and Science,
and they said anyone with eyes could see
that God was dead! So all of us were free
to idolize ourselves and have a go
at lives of self-indulgent self-reliance.
We mocked the silly rules that we were taught.
We said the only rule was, "Don't get caught."

We also said . . . Oh, sure, you do. Sit down.
Those tulips don't need help from you. We said
that "bad" means "good," that History is bunk,
and junk placed on a pedestal is Art.
Ah-hah, but speaking of, you've seen it, too—
that show of well-wrought turds at the museum.
The critics say the artist re-presents
the human figure from within. Don't laugh.
The guy gets serious money for his stuff
which shows it's Art. Come on, get with it, Mac,
Relax. I'm kidding you. His stuff is crap.

More than just the weather's changed this year.
I've talked to neighbors while we stood outside
before the open doors of our garages.
From time to time we looked up at the sky.
Why? Because we don't know what to do.
We can't believe the things we thought we knew,
which means that now we half-believe there's more
to life than having fun and keeping score.
Don't ask me what, but it's occurred to us
that things we cannot see or touch or even
talk about in ways that make much sense

like Beauty, Love and God are just as true
as what detectives count as evidence.
So once again, my friend, you are the time
"whanne longen folk to goon on pilgrimages."

In 1961, Piero Manzoni produced ninety cans of *Artist's Shit*. (Duchamp turned a toilet into Art; Manzoni followed up by turning the toilet's contents into Art.) Each of Manzoni's cans (the artistic word is "tins") is numbered on the lid 001 to 090.

The artist and critic Jon Thompson has written: "Manzoni's critical and metaphorical reification of the artist's body, its processes and products, pointed the way towards an understanding of the artist and the product of the artist's body as a consumable object."

Museums in London, Paris, and New York have bought cans of Manzoni's shit. Sotheby's sold one in 2007 for £124,000. And another in 2008 for £97,250. Christie's sold one in 2015 for £182,500. Alas, there is now some question about the contents of the cans. Do they contain the artist's shit or not? There is no way to be sure without destroying a work of art. The uncertainty, it is said "imbues" the cans "with an additional level of irony." (No shit.)